Neville,

So great m'
with your Looking .

Con th
of AHAs.

Write YOUR AHAbook Now!

Share one AHAmessage on social media from this AHAbook and receive a $100 discount when publishing your AHAbook on AHAthat.

Go to **http://aha.pub/AuthorPay** and enter the coupon code DYA100 to receive your discount of $100.

After your payment is made, go to **http://AHAthat.com/Author** and start writing your AHAbook.

Hey, Did You AHAthat?

Thought Leadership in Seven Seconds or Less!
Build Your Brand with AHAthat!

Mitchell Levy, Carly Alyssa Thorne, Jeff Shavitz, Dr. Tianna Conte, and Tiffany Vuong

An Actionable Business Journal

E-mail: info@thinkaha.com
20660 Stevens Creek Blvd., Suite 210
Cupertino, CA 95014

⇨ Please go to http://aha.pub/aha to read this AHAbook and to share the individual AHAmessages that resonate with you.

Published by THiNKaha®
20660 Stevens Creek Blvd., Suite 210, Cupertino, CA 95014
http://thinkaha.com
E-mail: info@thinkaha.com

First Printing: January 2017
Hardcover ISBN: 978-1-61699-201-9 (1-61699-201-8)
Paperback ISBN: 978-1-61699-200-2 (1-61699-200-X)
eBook ISBN: 978-1-61699-199-9 (1-61699-199-2)
Place of Publication: Silicon Valley, California, USA
Paperback Library of Congress Number: 2016915047

Trademarks

All terms mentioned in this book that are known to be trademarks or service marks have been appropriately capitalized. Neither THiNKaha, nor any of its imprints, can attest to the accuracy of this information. Use of a term in this book should not be regarded as affecting the validity of any trademark or service mark.

Warning and Disclaimer

Every effort has been made to make this book as complete and as accurate as possible. The information provided is on an "as is" basis. The author(s), publisher, and their agents assume no responsibility for errors or omissions. Nor do they assume liability or responsibility to any person or entity with respect to any loss or damages arising from the use of information contained herein.

Dedication

To Carly Alyssa Thorne, Jeff Shavitz, Tiffany Vuong, and Dr. Tianna Conte, who were interviewed for this book, and to all future AHAbook authors who use this approach or find other creative ways to write their AHAbooks.

What I Do

As the "AHA Guy," I love making people think—asking that one question or sharing that one story that will help you think about the world or solve a small problem/issue you have in a much different way.

I call these nuggets of thought "AHA" messages, as their goal is to produce AHA moments you act on when you're involved in a project or working on an idea. Taking it a step further, I want you to create your AHAmessages that you share with your audience to cause them to have their own AHA moments.

I speak at events and am brought in to facilitate groups and conduct one-on-one mentoring with those who want to create their brand, have their expertise known, and be recognized as thought leaders. I help them carve their target market into "reachable" chunks and focus on the tools they should be using to reach that market and hit their goals.

As a publisher, I assist individuals and organizations understand how they can amplify what they are doing to get more reach and engagement. One of the goals is to grow their fan base that will support their success while supporting themselves.

Instead of using the term "thought leader," I use the term "AHA leader." I believe that we all need to be AHA leaders. We all need to curate good, compelling content and share it with the audience that wants to receive it. The AHAthat platform is designed to help you. We have tens of thousands of curated AHAmessages that can be shared on social media for free in seconds.

The next step in being a recognized expert is to author a thought leader book. That's also where AHAthat comes in. I've pulled together a time-tested, proven process that hundreds of authors have used to write their AHAbooks in eight hours or less. If you have a skill and want to build your brand to serve an audience, you can reach that audience with a book that demonstrates that you're the expert.

The late Jay Conrad Levinson, the father of guerilla marketing, told me in an interview that "if there's a customer need, then a book can be used to show that you or your product can address it."

What I Know

Since 2005, my book publishing firm, THiNKaha, has produced over 800 books. I was told back then that the book business was dying. It's not. I've also been told that thought leadership is an overused term and it's dying. It's not. Another wrong I've heard involves social media. I've been told that social media doesn't work. That's wrong, it does.

With our success, I knew that if I wanted to convince others to create their AHAbooks, I needed to create one myself on why anyone would want to create an AHAbook. I decided to demonstrate this by interviewing others who are familiar with the platform. To that end, I know how to interview thought leaders and repurpose the content from those interviews in several different formats. This knowledge comes from running the show "Thought Leader Life" (**http://ThoughtLeaderLife**). At "Thought Leader Life," we parse the AHA moments from four to five thirty-minute shows to create an AHAbook.

This is how this book was created, and it addresses the who, what, where, when, why, and how of writing an AHAbook. The AHAmessages in this book came from the following interviews with four of our amazing authors and are available on YouTube or through the Thought Leader Life channel:

- Mitchell Levy diatribe: **http://aha.pub/ahaMitchellVideo**
- w/ Carly Alyssa Thorne: **http://aha.pub/ahaCarlyVideo**
- w/ Tiffany Vuong: **http://aha.pub/ahaTiffanyVideo**
- w/ Dr. Tianna Conte: **http://aha.pub/ahaTiannaVideo**
- w/ Jeff Shavitz: **http://aha.pub/ahaJeffVideo**

What is a book? For me, as a publisher of over 800 books, a book is a tool that should be used to demonstrate your expertise. Even better, it's a tool that should be used to generate one or more AHA moments in your reader. What better way to inspire than to have a book of 140 potential AHA moments that will positively affect your audience, whether they read any one of those AHAmessages directly in your AHAbook or somewhere on social media.

I know that if you want to demonstrate your skill or that of a product to be used to solve a problem, an AHAbook is the tool that can be used to do it quickly and easily. I also know that some people would prefer physical books instead of eBooks. That's the cool part. You write your AHAbook in eight hours or less and then have us turn that book into PDF, Kindle, paperback, and hardcover formats. Very easy—very powerful.

What I Want

I want you to be successful. I want you to communicate effectively in a way that your existing and future fans understand who you are and what you stand for. I want those fans to appreciate the content you curate and originate and to share that content with their networks. Make sense? You share content with your current audience and some of them will share it with their audience and so on, which helps both audiences grow.

I want you to understand the value of an AHAbook and how to explain it in relation to two other eBook formats. For simplicity, let's say there are three types of eBook formats. First is PDF, which is a single file that is typically read online or sent to your local printing device to read. The second is ePub, which is the format typically sent to Amazon to load into the Kindle platform. The third type of eBook format is an AHAbook, which is a social media-enabled eBook containing 140 AHAmessages, where every AHAmessage is instantly shareable at a click of a button to Twitter, Facebook, LinkedIn, and Google+.

Social media and thought leadership are going to be around for a while. For the naysayers, let's say five years. For others, let's say a decade or a century or a couple of centuries. I lean toward the latter. If that's the case, why don't you use a platform designed to optimize both areas! AHAthat is sparking a revolutionary time-to-market concept in marketing and branding.

I want to see you write and use the AHAthat platform as a tool to accomplish your goals and find new and unique ways to create and share your AHAmessages. Everyone who reads the content you share (yours and others), as well as everyone who finds and shares your content to their networks, are potential customers.

This book was created through interviews and published as an AHAbook that can be seen at http://aha.pub/aha. After that, it was turned into a PDF, Kindle, paperback and hardcover version. The interview approach represents one way of writing your AHAbook. After reading all or a small portion of this book, I want to see you get excited about writing your AHAbook in eight hours or less. You up for the challenge? Trust me, once you see how easy it is to do one and experience the results we've seen achieved by many of our authors, you are going to write more.

How to Read a THiNKaha® Book
A Note from the Publisher

The THiNKaha series is the CliffsNotes of the 21st century. The value of these books is that they are contextual in nature. Although the actual words won't change, their meaning will change every time you read one as your context will change. Experience your own "AHA!" moments ("AHAmessages™") with a THiNKaha book; AHAmessages are looked at as "actionable" moments—think of a specific project you're working on, an event, a sales deal, a personal issue, etc. and see how the AHAmessages in this book can inspire your own AHAmessages, something that you can specifically act on. Here's how to read one of these books and have it work for you:

1. Read a THiNKaha book (these slim and handy books should only take about 15–20 minutes of your time!) and write down one to three actionable items you thought of while reading it. Each journal-style THiNKaha book is equipped with space for you to write down your notes and thoughts underneath each AHAmessage.

2. Mark your calendar to re-read this book again in 30 days.

3. Repeat step #1 and write down one to three more AHAmessages that grab you this time. I guarantee that they will be different than the first time. BTW: this is also a great time to reflect on the actions taken from the last set of AHAmessages you wrote down.

After reading a THiNKaha book, writing down your AHAmessages, re-reading it, and writing down more AHAmessages, you'll begin to see how these books contextually apply to you. THiNKaha books advocate for continuous, lifelong learning. They will help you transform your AHAs into actionable items with tangible results until you no longer have to say "AHA!" to these moments—they'll become part of your daily practice as you continue to grow and learn.

As The AHA Guy at THiNKaha, I definitely practice what I preach. I read 2-3 AHAbooks a month in addition to those that we publish and take away two to three different action items from each of them every time. Please e-mail me your AHAs today!

Mitchell Levy
publisher@thinkaha.com

Contents

Section 1

Demonstrating Your Expertise
Is Changing

Want to press the "easy" button on writing a book?
Writing a book is hard—extremely hard. Pushing yourself
to sit down, deliberate, write, edit, rewrite, put heads
together again, and then rewrite some more until you
reach between 15,000–100,000 words is such punishing
and exhausting work, isn't it? Now here comes a new
platform called AHAthat (**http://AHAthat.com**),
where you can write a book in eight hours or less. AHAthat
makes it easy to SHARE, AUTHOR, and PROMOTE
yourself (i.e. your brand). It is the first AHAleadership
(Thought Leadership) platform on the market. With
AHAthat, you can show your "worldliness" by sharing
curated content of other thought leaders, and you can
easily demonstrate your expertise by quickly writing your
AHAbook and making it easy for you and others to share
your content.

1

If you want to capture the reader's attention today, you need to do it in seven seconds or less. Are you doing that? @HappyAbout

_____

_____

_____

2

An authentic and effective way to introduce your business to people is: writing a book. You only need 8 hours. @CarlyAThorne

_____

_____

_____

3

Social media is a "we" conversation. If you are just broadcasting, you are talking about "I." That won't work. @CarlyAThorne

_____

_____

_____

4

Traditional publishing is at the bottom of the spiral. Long production time, and most royalties are a pittance. @DrTianna

_____

_____

_____

5

How can you go beyond the traditional way people think about books? Try an AHAbook on http://AHAthat.com. @CarlyAThorne

---

6

We need to have 80% of our content come from others. Where else can you find that content? http://AHAthat.com
@CarlyAThorne

_____

_____

_____

7

One idea can change your life and change the world. What's your idea? Make it happen now! http://AHAthat.com/Author @DrTianna

_____

_____

_____

Section II

Who Are AHAleaders and Can You Become One?

AHAleaders (known as Thought Leaders) are your own personal curators. They help you press the "easy" button by sharing their wisdom that applies to you. They are those people who tell you what's happening in the marketplace and share a solution that they think will give your current situation a fix. They keep themselves informed and maintain a closer relationship with their audience. Who are the AHAleaders you like, trust, respect, and follow?

8

An AHAleader is your own personal curator. Who's yours? @HappyAbout

_____

_____

_____

9

AHAleaders are curators who listen to their customers' problems and give appropriate answers. @HappyAbout

_____

_____

_____

10

An AHAleader should be familiar with their peers and the marketplace. Are you aware of your surroundings? @HappyAbout

_____

_____

_____

11

AHAleaders are #Authentic, #Transparent, and #Trustworthy. Are you an AHAleader? @HappyAbout

_____

_____

_____

12

With AHAthat, you can quote other people and by doing so, increase your "AHAleaderness" and your ability to succeed. @HappyAbout

_____

_____

_____

13

It's easier to trust someone who's selling if they can put their service in the context of their peers. #AHAleader @HappyAbout

_____

_____

_____

Section III: What Is an AHAbook?

Section III

What Is an AHAbook?

An AHAbook gives you credibility. An AHAbook allows you to focus on a specialized topic and demonstrate expertise in that topic. An AHAbook with AHAthat has easily shareable content for Twitter, Facebook, LinkedIn, and Google+. AHAbooks are comprised of 140 bite-sized quotes that are motivating, compelling, and influencing. It allows individuals, businessmen, authors, and even students to advance and explore their creativity as content creators. Author your own social media-enabled book today!

14

AHAthat as a platform can bestow integrity, value, and AHAleadership. Are you using it? http://AHAthat.com @HappyAbout

---

15

An AHAbook brands your uniqueness. People spend a fortune to get branded, whereas one AHAbook can brand you. #WOW @DrTianna

16

I don't have the time anymore to take a year to write a 200-page book. AHAbooks are just 140 thoughts. http://AHAthat.com/Author @JeffShavitz

---

17

If you don't want to be in social media but know you need to, here is a way. http://AHAthat.com takes care of SMM. @JeffShavitz

18

AHAbooks create a platform because they're tidbits of wisdom that are then shared on social media. It's #brilliant! @DrTianna

_____

_____

_____

19

With every quote you create in an AHAbook, you add your Twitter handle, which gives you attribution for that quote.
@CarlyAThorne

_____

_____

_____

20

AHAmessages are easy to "Grab and Share" on your blog posts, presentations, social media, etc. Why not share now? @HappyAbout

---

21

AHAbooks are for the early adopters, the trailblazers, the visionaries who want to play bigger in the world. @DrTianna

22

Every business person has to have a platform for their customers and employees. This is what an AHAbook can do for you.
@HappyAbout

_____

_____

_____

23

Your goal in any conversation is to create
an AHA moment. What better way than
with a platform focused on AHAs!
@CarlyAThorne

_____

_____

_____

24

You can read AHAmessages through
AHAthat, Kindle, and physical books!
Which do you prefer? Share an AHA today!
@HappyAbout

_____

_____

_____

25

There are many interesting AHAbooks
you can read & share in #AHAthat, which
will keep your audience stimulated.
@CarlyAThorne

_____

_____

_____

26

AHAthat is not about a book, it's about a movement. It's a ripple effect to help experts share their expertise. @DrTianna

---

27

The best medium to write quotes for #SocialMedia, #Branding, and #Marketing is an AHAbook on http://AHAthat.com. @CarlyAThorne

---

28

With AHAbooks, the authors are giving you permission to share their content with attribution. We want you to share!
@HappyAbout

_____

_____

_____

29

An AHAbook is for credibility. It's more like a business card than a book. It goes way beyond a business card on social.
@DrTianna

_____

_____

_____

30

AHAbooks provide easily digestible, valuable content for readers of similar interest. Have you read & shared one? @CarlyAThorne

_____

_____

_____

31

AHAthat offers easy access and is fun and simple, so it's easy to muster the courage to take the first step. @DrTianna

---

32

AHAbooks provide a rich source of compelling content you can share in bite-sized quotes. What's your AHA today? @CarlyAThorne

---

33

AHAbooks give people a taste.
If they want to go deeper,
then they can go deeper.
http://AHAthat.com @DrTianna

_____

_____

_____

34

AHAmessages on @AHAthat are pithy, concise, and to the point, which readers can easily understand. http://AHAthat.com
@CarlyAThorne

_____

_____

_____

35

An AHAbook is the key message that you're about. The brilliance of coupling it with social media is a new pathway.
@DrTianna

_____

_____

_____

36

Use amazing quotes from #AHAthat
authors to express your expertise
and your passion to others.
@CarlyAThorne

_____

_____

_____

37

An AHAbook is easy to produce, fun to read, and fast to share its bite-sized tidbits of wisdom. @DrTianna

_____

_____

_____

Section IV

Why Should You Create an AHAbook Today?

Creating an AHAbook helps you build your brand and grow your business. It's a great way to get your content out there quickly and spread by your fanbase and beyond. AHAbooks are the easiest way to hit the "easy" button on writing your book. It helps you increase your influence, leverage information, and get in touch with the community by sharing inspiring and valuable bite-sized quotes. It serves as a significant step on your route toward AHAleadership. When will you start building your own AHAbook?

38

With an AHAbook, you are not
writing it to solve world hunger,
you are writing it to target customer #1.
http://AHAthat.com/Author @HappyAbout

_____

_____

_____

39

With AHAbooks, people can get great content the way they are outlined. They are very thought-provoking. @JeffShavitz

---

40

With one unique idea, an AHAbook can brand a person as a credible expert. @DrTianna

_____

_____

_____

41

If you want to differentiate yourself in the market, AHAbooks is a way, at a reasonable price, to get yourself out there. @JeffShavitz

_____

_____

_____

42

The quickest anyone has written an #AHAbook is @JoelComm, who spent 20 minutes reviewing comments from his Facebook post. @HappyAbout

---

43

With AHAbooks, an idea becomes formed from spirit and then forms to function, making a difference in people's lives. @DrTianna

---

44

My AHAbooks have changed my life in so many ways. It has opened up many doors for me. What will it do for you? @JeffShavitz

_____

_____

_____

45

AHAbooks are essentially like workbooks. They are interactive compared to reading a novel. @JeffShavitz

_____

_____

_____

46

Writing my AHAbook is a tool that will help me going forward in my career. @TiffanyVuong

---

47

Longing to make a difference in your family's lives and the lives of others? An AHAbook is an easy step. @DrTianna

---

48

The world is so cluttered with so many messages, how will you stand out? You stand out by writing an AHAbook.
@HappyAbout

_____

_____

_____

49

If you're introverted and you need an excuse to reach out to people, writing an AHAbook is a great one. @TiffanyVuong

---

50

With AHAbooks, your wisdom can touch people even without you being there. #ThatsThePoint @DrTianna

---

51

Today, there are many ways to creatively introduce your biz to others; write an AHAbook in 8 hours. @CarlyAThorne

_____

_____

_____

52

AHAbooks have very actionable content, whereas traditional books are just informative. http://AHAthat.com @JeffShavitz

_____

_____

_____

53

It was a really great experience for me to write an AHAbook. You should too. http://AHAthat.com/Author @TiffanyVuong

_____

_____

_____

54

AHAbooks transform the way we think about helping people build their character and value. @HappyAbout

_____

_____

_____

55

If you are out there selling your services, there is no better tool to open doors than interviewing prospects for a book. @HappyAbout

_____

_____

_____

56

With a book, you now have an income-generating asset for the rest of your life. @JeffShavitz

_____

_____

_____

57

With AHAbooks, you can write about anything, and I think it would be a good experience for anybody to write one. @TiffanyVuong

_____

_____

_____

58

I see so much benefit with AHAbooks,
I collaborated with my teenage daughter
so she can be an author and speak
on her book. @JeffShavitz

_____

_____

_____

59

Extend your business model by writing an AHAbook with (and for) your clients. Think of the impact it will have. @HappyAbout

_____

_____

_____

60

You can really take ownership that you're
the expert of whatever field as the
author of an AHAbook. @JeffShavitz

_____

_____

_____

61

The concept of writing an AHAbook book
is a good thing. I did it. You can write on
any topic. What's yours? @TiffanyVuong

_____

_____

_____

62

Creating AHAbooks is not just about the money. It's also about meeting people and building relationships. @JeffShavitz

---

63

A CEO co-writing an AHAbook with their employees is a more personal experience that helps employees get engaged.
@HappyAbout

_____

_____

_____

64

AHAbooks are quickies. They are fast to produce and fast to read and fast to share on social. @DrTianna

_____

_____

_____

65

Writing an AHAbook forces the author to focus on the most relevant impactful thoughts in that space. @JeffShavitz

_____

_____

_____

66

Want to build your character, your
perceived value among your perspective
clients? Write an AHAbook in 8 hours.
@JeffShavitz

_____

_____

_____

67

AHAbooks give people momentum to go farther -- freeing their unique gift for that global ripple effect. @DrTianna

---

68

Co-writing an AHAbook is collaborative, where you help the other person have the tools to learn, experiment, and grow. @HappyAbout

---

69

If you don't take a step, nothing happens.
So the AHAbook is the first step
toward a movement. @DrTianna

_____

_____

_____

70

Writing an AHAbook is easy, simple,
straightforward. It takes only 8 steps.
http://AHAthat.com/Author
@HappyAbout @TiffanyVuong

_____

_____

_____

71

The book that took me a couple hundred hours to write isn't read in its entirety. My AHAbooks are. Much more powerful! @JeffShavitz

_____

_____

_____

72

Take an AHA step, and your world
will open up to a new paradigm of
publishing possibilities. @DrTianna

_____

_____

_____

73

You can become the recognized expert in your chosen field if you write an AHAbook on that specific field. @JeffShavitz

_____

_____

_____

74

If you become an author, you have to be a marketer too. You have to know what to do with your books. @JeffShavitz

_____

_____

_____

75

Author an AHAbook to discuss the problem your business solves. It's better than biz cards & flyers! @CarlyAThorne

_____

_____

_____

Section V

How Can You Easily Create an AHAbook?

The AHAthat platform has intrinsic qualities that make the process of writing an AHAbook as smooth and efficient as possible. If you are going to attend a conference, conduct an interview, send out a survey, or are being hit by that *AHA moment,* you can write a treatise about it. As long as you are passionate about writing what you love, creating it is just like letting beautiful pearls of wisdom slip from your mouth. On what topic would you like to write an AHAbook?

76

Just start. Write the book. Write the first AHA. Then continue. Whether it's 1 a week or 5 a week, you will get better at it. @JeffShavitz

_____

_____

_____

77

You can capture the reader's attention based on the headline you use. Start using catchy ones, it's fun and beneficial! @HappyAbout

_____

_____

_____

78

AHAbooks contain digestible quotes, which are different from the typical quotes you have seen before. Agreed? @CarlyAThorne

---

79

Who is your market? How you write your quotes should be in a way that will reach the "right audience." @TiffanyVuong

_____

_____

_____

80

Make your thoughts so concise to fit 140 characters. Think carefully about what's most important in your chosen field. @JeffShavitz

_____

_____

_____

81

As quick as you can write an AHAbook,
why not consider writing one with the
intent of picking up that one "key" client.
@HappyAbout

82

As you write and learn the system, it's like
any muscle. It gets better with time and you
get more comfortable writing. @JeffShavitz

83

Two hours of recorded content is all you need to create an AHAbook. It's amazing how easy it is. #EasyButton. @HappyAbout

_____

_____

_____

84

You are great at something. Just pick the subject, write the book, and it will open doors you would have never imagined.
@JeffShavitz

85

I used hashtags not only to wrap up, but to add humor to the quotes. What are you gonna do with your AHAbook?
@TiffanyVuong

86

Just get started. That's the key thing. Just take a step. Any step. You can't go on a journey unless you take a step. @DrTianna

_____

_____

_____

87

AHAthat has a rich source of good quality bite-sized quotes that are easy to share. I love the platform. @CarlyAThorne

_____

_____

_____

88

Your AHAbook doesn't always have to be serious. You can write light and funny topics that appeal to your audience. @CarlyAThorne

_____

_____

_____

89

Are you thinking of a subject to write on? Write an AHAbook on where you want to generate business tomorrow. @HappyAbout

_____

_____

_____

90

What is your market? How do you reach it?
How do you relate to it? Interviewing folks
for your AHAbook will help. @HappyAbout

_____

_____

_____

91

Interviewing others doesn't always create
good content. It's okay to make it better.
Prep your Interviewees ahead of time.
@TiffanyVuong

_____

_____

_____

92

Finding it hard thinking about a topic for your AHAbook? Think about your target audience and what problem they want solved. @HappyAbout

_____

_____

_____

93

Anyone can write their own AHAbook.
If you are passionate about it,
then go for it! @CarlyAThorne

_____

_____

_____

94

Once you've written an AHAbook, the next thing to consider is who you can help write their AHAbook. Powerful bonding! @HappyAbout

_____

_____

_____

95

Want to better capture the attention of your target audience? Turn your AHAbooks into paperback and hardcover editions. @HappyAbout

_____

_____

_____

96

Imagine someone has a problem. Now write a new AHAbook that solves that problem. Then do it again. @DrTianna

_____

_____

_____

97

You can author an AHAbook based on your notes from a conference in just 2-3 hours. What's your next conference? @HappyAbout

_____

_____

_____

98

You can write an AHAbook to raise
awareness on an alarming topic.
You and the topic will receive attention.
@CarlyAThorne

99

Use a similar hashtag in every quote so you can listen when people are sharing your content, and respond appropriately.
@HappyAbout

_____

_____

_____

100

The question about takeaways & your market is helpful to think about before you actually write something. @TiffanyVuong

_____

_____

_____

101

In writing an AHAbook, it is important that you pick a topic you're passionate about and will inspire readers. @CarlyAThorne

_____

_____

_____

102

You have to be very careful to give attribution when sharing content. That's why sharing from @AHAthat is great. #WeDoIt @HappyAbout

_____

_____

_____

103

One idea turns into one AHA moment for an author. Then it's easy. Take the step to start your AHAbook today. @DrTianna

_____

_____

_____

104

In writing an AHAbook, you should think about content that other people will want to share with their tribe. @HappyAbout

_____

_____

_____

105

You have to think out of the box to
make an authentic AHAbook. You can!
Just be yourself! Write it from the heart.
@CarlyAThorne

_____

_____

_____

106

After writing a couple of books for the
AHAthat platform, it only takes me
2 hours to write an AHAbook. Crazy, right?
@CarlyAThorne

_____

_____

_____

107

Just because a speaker shared copyrighted
content publicly doesn't mean you can
use it without the appropriate attribution.
@HappyAbout

_____

_____

_____

108

Once I wrote the summary and thought
about how I was going to section it off,
the topic of my book became clear to me.
@TiffanyVuong

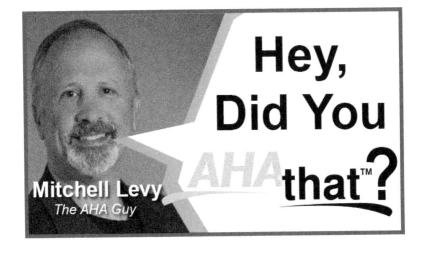

Section VI

Hey, Did You AHAthat?

Each of us has exciting stories to tell, from challenges we have overcome to uplifting lessons we've learned from our experiences. All these things are worth sharing to people who we believe might benefit from these feverish bits and pieces. What are the things or topics that get you excited? Did you AHAthat? If not, then you should!

109

What comes to mind when you hear the phrase "Social Media-Enabled eBook?" Share your thoughts! @HappyAbout

_____

_____

_____

110

If you're networking, it's great to have a reason to reach out to people. Write an AHAbook. #BreakTheIce. @TiffanyVuong

_____

_____

_____

111

There are many different authors. How will you stand out? #AHAbooks #AHAmovement @DrTianna

_____

_____

_____

112

If you're a CEO, why are you not helping
your employees be more successful? One
way is through a vehicle like an AHAbook.
@HappyAbout

_____

_____

_____

113

Once I touched on something, I didn't want to repeat it because I wanted to save that space for a new thought. #AHAmessages @TiffanyVuong

114

You will be seen on social as you and others share your compelling, heartfelt AHAmessages via @AHAthat. @CarlyAThorne

115

How powerful would your company be if all your employees had an AHAbook on a topic they were expert in? @HappyAbout

_____

_____

_____

116

How do you want to help the people who read your book? #MakeItEasy @TiffanyVuong

_____

_____

_____

117

Imagine being given an AHAbook by a person who's empowering you w/ their message; it will touch your soul. @DrTianna

_____

_____

_____

118

You need to be searchable, you need to be
recognizable, you need to share content.
Otherwise, you don't exist. @CarlyAThorne

_____

_____

_____

119

As an introvert, it's hard for me to reach out to people, but once you have a cause for reaching out, it becomes easier.
@TiffanyVuong

_____

_____

_____

120

Everybody's got a book inside them.
What's yours? #SelfBranding @DrTianna

_____

_____

_____

121

You should be able to talk about your
accomplishments. You should be able to be
proud of what you're doing. @TiffanyVuong

_____

_____

_____

122

Who are you? What is your unique gift that you can give to the planet that only you are uniquely qualified to give? @DrTianna

_____

_____

_____

123

It's easy to post about your accomplishments w/ social media. It's easy to put out there what you've been doing. @TiffanyVuong

_____

_____

_____

124

What do you want your readers to
take away from your book? What is your
overall message? @TiffanyVuong

_____

_____

_____

125

I have an AHA, now AHAthat.
Did you AHAthat? @CarlyAThorne

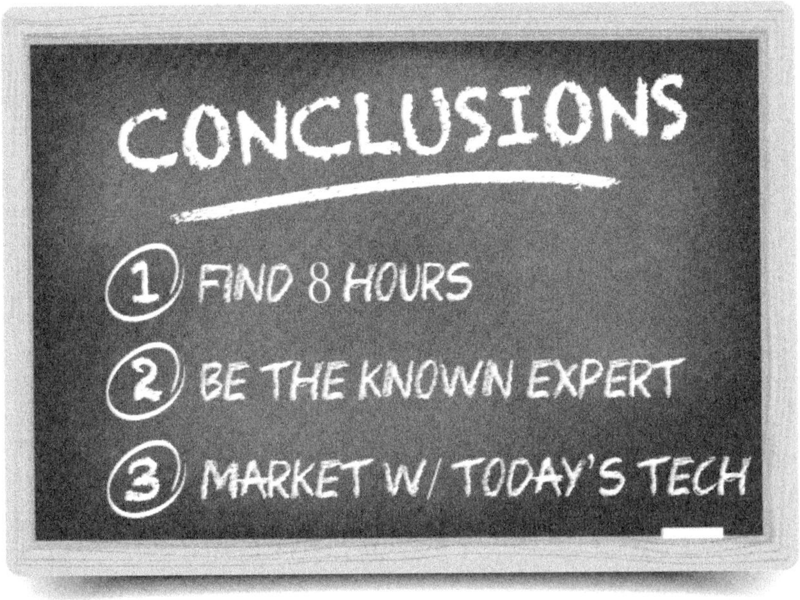
CONCLUSIONS
1 FIND 8 HOURS
2 BE THE KNOWN EXPERT
3 MARKET W/ TODAY'S TECH

Section VII

Conclusion

Writing an AHAbook in AHAthat is a splendid way to share enlightening and insightful quotes or AHAmessages about a particular topic. These aren't just ordinary quotes; these are messages that impose soundness and give answers or solutions to readers' problems. They don't just inspire; they also help. It's the next big thing that makes a significant impact using the least amount of time, effort, and money. Make your book come to life, and engage more of your followers today!

126

It's fun to write an AHAbook. It's a very simple format. Just sit down and start. Get the book done! @JeffShavitz

_____

_____

_____

127

With an AHAbook, you cement your relationship with your audience and your readers, and you stand out of the crowd. @HappyAbout

_____

_____

_____

128

With the AHAbook author being given
51% of the profits, the author is given more
honor. It's a win-win-win situation.
@DrTianna

_____

_____

_____

129

AHAbooks are on top of the spiral as
they take the least amount of time, energy,
and money. #BrandYourself @DrTianna

_____

_____

_____

130

With AHAbooks, you're free with money,
you're free with time, and you've got a
platform. What are you waiting for?
@DrTianna

_____

_____

_____

131

With AHAthat, you don't have to wait a year or 2 to do a book. You can do a new book every quarter, focusing on a new niche.
@HappyAbout

_____

_____

_____

132

See what idea, your AHA, you want to be known for, and brand yourself now rather than later. @DrTianna

_____

_____

_____

133

Many people don't have the time to actually read a full book, whereas they can read an AHAbook in 10 to 20 minutes. @JeffShavitz

134

It's not just about what we do, it's about the impact of what we do. @AHAthat helps you create the impact. @CarlyAThorne

135

It'll be a good experience for anybody to write an AHAbook. Whatever you're interested in, you can write about it. @TiffanyVuong

_____

_____

_____

136

There should be an AHAbook for every life event, an AHAbook in every household. @HappyAbout

---

137

The ROI on a book is huge. Giving your prospect your soundbites can close business. @CarlyAThorne

---

138

AHAthat is so easy & painless. It blesses people faster. Producing an AHAbook is fun. Bite-sized things are fun! @DrTianna

_____

_____

_____

139

Write an AHAbook and you will be
transformed. Your confidence level will
increase and it will take you forward in life.
@HappyAbout

140

AHAbooks is the next evolutionary step,
the next big thing. Don't procrastinate!
Create your AHAbook now. @DrTianna

About the Authors

MITCHELL LEVY

Mitchell Levy @HappyAbout is the CEO and Thought Leader Architect at THiNKaha and The AHA Guy at AHAthat. He and his team make it easy for corporations to create compelling content that helps turn their experts into recognized thought leaders.

CARLY ALYSSA THORNE

....

Carly Alyssa Thorne is a speaker, author, consultant, producer, and director on Conscious Business Collaborations, specializing in multisensory, multimedia, and the mind-body-business-spirit interconnectedness. She also has an extended background in metaphysics and health, having owned and consulted in several healing centers.

JEFF SHAVITZ

....

Jeff Shavitz is the CEO of TrafficJamming, a virtual membership group for business owners and entrepreneurs, comprised of many business services to help drive customers to their companies. He is a serial entrepreneur who has written four business books, including *Size Doesn't Matter —Why Small Business Is BIG Business*, which hit No.1 on Amazon.

DR. TIANNA CONTE

....

Dr. Tianna Conte @DrTianna is an energetic, passionate, and seasoned Self-Evolution Mentor. She is a unique blend of mystic and scientist whose childhood mystical roots led to a career that has spanned over 25 years as a trained Naturopath, Ordained Interfaith Minster, and initiated Shaman. Her passion is in integrating ancient healing wisdom and cutting-edge technologies in energy mastery.

TIFFANY VUONG

....

Tiffany Vuong @TiffanyVuong is currently an undergraduate student at San Jose State University, majoring in industrial and systems engineering with a minor in business. She was the Vice President of Communications in AIESEC, the largest student-run organization in the world, is currently the Executive Vice President of the Institute for Industrial Engineers, and is on the organizational committee to hosting the first Spartan-Hacks: Civic Tech competition at SJSU. She is the author of the AHAbook *Millennial Pet Peeves*.

AHAthat™

AHAthat makes it easy to share, author, and promote content. There are over 35,000 quotes (AHAmessages™) by thought leaders from around the world that you can share in seconds for free.

For those who want to author their own book, we have time-tested proven processes that allow you to write your AHAbook™ of 140 digestible, bite-sized morsels in eight hours or less. Once your content is on AHAthat, you have a customized link that you can use to have your fans/advocates share your content and help grow your network.

⟳ Start sharing: **http://AHAthat.com**

⟳ Start authoring: **http://AHAthat.com/Author**

Please go directly to this book in AHAthat and share each AHAmessage socially at **http://aha.pub/aha**.

Get Your Own Customized Book

Imagine sharing a business card that will sit on your prospect's desk for years. A physical book is that business card! You pick any book in our inventory and tell us how we can customize it for your use.

With your customized book:

- You get a book of over 100 quotes that reference you.

- You get a customized URL that can be used by you and others to share these quotes.

- You will have a great lead generator that will significantly increase social media traffic to you.

- In addition to a reference to you on the cover, you have a page inside the book with a personalized message designed to appeal to your customers and prospects.

- Your photo and bio will be used on the back cover and inside the book.

Want More Info? Contact THiNKaha
(**CustomBooks@thinkaha.com**, 408-257-3000).

Be Associated with a
Legendary Thought Leader

Imagine being associated with one of your favorite thought leaders whose content is in the public domain. We've created 140 quotes from their public domain books and can associate you with them in either online or physical book form. Want to get yours too?

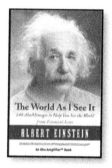  

Check out **http://aha.pub/PublicDomain**
for our growing library of public domain books.

Want More Info? Contact THiNKaha
(**CustomBooks@thinkaha.com**, 408-257-3000).

Own a Phrase,
Make It Your Own!

Is there a phrase that you're known for or want to be known for? Want us to create a social media-enabled eBook and physical book for you with that phrase in 100+ languages?

Check out **http://aha.pub/Phrases** for our
growing library of phrase books.

Want More Info? Contact THiNKaha
(**http://aha.pub/PublicDomain**, 408-257-3000).

CPSIA information can be obtained
at www.ICGtesting.com
Printed in the USA
FSOW03n0632090217
30547FS